AF571993

INFINITY in the PALM of ONE'S HAND

Poems by

Robert H. Deluty

GATEWAY PRESS, INC.
Baltimore, MD 2006

Please direct all correspondence and book orders to:
Robert H. Deluty
4783 Ilkley Moor Lane
Ellicott City, Maryland 21043

Library of Congress Control Number 2006928260

ISBN-10 0-9704201-2-9
ISBN-13 9780970420121

Published by
Gateway Press, Inc.
3600 Clipper Mill Rd., Suite 260
Baltimore, MD 21211-1953

Printed in the United States of America

To

Ronald Pies, Richard Berlin,
Clarinda Harriss, David Barlow,
Robert Rosenthal, Cyril Franks,
Miryam Wahrman, Alan Kazdin,
Kathy Kubala, & Alyce Hershenhart

Other books by Robert H. Deluty
published by Gateway Press

Within and Between: Poems (2000)
The Long and Short of It: Essays and Poems (2003)
Observed and Imagined: Poems and Essays (2004)
The Essence of Moments: Poems (2004)
Treasuring the Details: Poems (2005)
Present Sense: New and Selected Poems (2005)
Glimpses and Snapshots: Poems (2005)
Specks and Flashes: Poems (2006)

Contents

8 an accordion
ancient Greek scholars
in an ER
his grandfather
her son arguing

9 2:40 a.m.
OCD woman
a two-year-old boy
midsummer day
a sixteen-year-old

10 health food store owner
their fourth meeting
circus performer
backyard hammock
three men in a bar

11 medieval scholar
an old poor woman
Jewish matron
post bachelor party
televangelist

12 her six-year-old
his kid sister calls
old janitor
centenarian
St. Patrick's Day

13 a boy practicing
elderly waiter
talentless actor
grandfather, grandson
in a deep sleep

14 with an eraser
their third session
ninety-year-old twins
field hockey star
theater district

15 married thirty years
a six-year-old girl
barber shop
March seventeenth
Baylor-DePaul game

16 school bus driver
post-circus
breakfast meeting
at the beach
frigid battlefield

17 in his office
Thanksgiving night
rural driver
math professor
from their bedrooms

18 Macular Degeneration

19 sub-zero night
married three weeks
in church, four brothers
uninsured man
an eighteen-year-old

20 bulimic teen
a young priest
paraplegic man
history teacher
overturned car

30 elderly driver
anxious defendant
young physician
Muslim cab driver
outside a classroom

31 drafting her vita
prepubescent boy
recent college grad
his blind date
grandmother's smile

32 college football fan
their five-year-old
stoic waitress
asked to describe
a house divided

33 during Passover
approaching a dwarf
infant twins' father
after her shift
little league shortstop

34 a French linguist
their teenaged son
3:10 a.m.
Easter Sunday
at the altar

35 third-rate writer
with a stepladder
CEO's desk
ESL class
her Hindu in-laws

36 on the beach
funeral service
great-grandmother
married six decades
golf foursome

37 trying to undo
Bronx graduation
book jacket photo
a burn victim
Saudi husband

38 Wyoming highway
their nine-year-old
using sugar cubes
before his orals
in the front row

39 a day off from school
old podiatrist
a germ-phobic man
Friday the thirteenth
an obese mailman

40 the night of the prom
an English teacher
fastidious Dad
depressing birthday
V.A. hospital

41 having crammed all night
their son's decision
on his deathbed
a Catholic boy
prison mess hall

42 an estranged son
church collection plate
Sunday evening
a poetess
a three-year-old's Mom

43 grad school applicant
an eighth grader
acrophobic man
family road trip
a nine-year-old girl

45 *Quotations (Samuel Johnson; Anais Nin)*

47 beleaguered father
paging the realtor
turnpike rest stop
teenaged Goth
his seven-year-old

48 Miami Beach
his psychologist
Jewish ten-year-old
inner city
his ex-wife's lisp

49 trying to recall
watching his girlfriend
sending off his child
at the Preakness
her son, asleep

50 on vacation
enraged father
Daytona Beach
a Marine's daughter
Passover's third night

51 a six-year-old boy
champion swimmer
fast food carry-out
bald-headed elder
a grieving child

52 old Bostonian
on a salesman's desk
post-vacation
in a storm cellar
unhelpful sales clerk

53 her three-year-old
New York tourist
his vintage sedan
baseball manager
old-fashioned father

54 her new son-in-law
on the expressway
Yom Kippur morning
little leaguer
a hole in his sock

55 young soccer goalie
a Brooklyn boy
her prom night
explains to his son
first-time shoplifter

56 finding their niche
movie night (I)
movie night (II)
teenager's father
Father's Day eve

57 after a hard day
M.B.A. student
trying to save gas
beloved elder
a police captain

58 middle-aged woman
reunion
abusive parents
in a batting slump
renowned novelist

59 math professor's son
treasuring the eyes
two rottweiler heads
deceased Mets fan
small town bus driver

61 *Quotations (Edna St. Vincent Millay; Oscar Wilde)*

63 Nobel laureate
fifth grade class photo
English professor
Jewish punk rocker
GRE morning

64 a ten-year-old boy
his mother
her teenaged son
psychotic patients
Auschwitz survivor

65 Christmas eve
his new girlfriend
bulimic student
parent/teacher night
senryu writer

66 dermatologist
Special Olympics
three preschoolers
his son's pet mouse
poor, depressed woman

67 mayoral debate
a rich man's mother
photographer
vet's office
lesbian's father

68 middle school bee
at the racetrack
four beagles
a renowned scholar
couples therapist

69 their twelve-year-old
a Hebrew School class
first-year grad student
wishing he had
his wife's father

70 an upscale teen
midnight, in prison
Boston socialist
a ten-year-old girl
elderly priest

71 high school recital
new father holding
hot summer evening
post-rhinoplasty
south Miami

72 at the M.V.A.
Berkeley faculty
dining with his son
a therapist frets
pugnacious chemist

73 thirtieth birthday
at the market
trying to find
the band playing
outside their school

74 uptown bar
a lawyer writing
four-year-old twins
young psychiatrist
a Jewish comic

75 owner of four cats
graduation day
a burly trucker
the Hoyle family
pre-wedding, the groom

76 psychoanalyst
Little Italy
family dinner
their Mom's funeral
a nine-year-old cook

77 classics professor
Utah leftist
outdoor commencement
an eight-year-old boy
burned-out therapist

Infinity
in the Palm
of One's Hand

To see a World in a Grain of Sand
And a Heaven in a Wild Flower,
Hold Infinity in the palm of your hand
And Eternity in an hour.

William Blake

a Jewish convert
in labor, delivering
her first *oy*

nonconformists
giving their newborn twin sons
different last names

her fifth birthday …
nearing the candles, wishing
for smaller ears

a new waiter
cursing out the old lady
who left him pennies

mid-June afternoon …
a young squirrel flirting
with a garden gnome

psychotic man
ruing the night he spurned
Sophia Loren

retirement home …
trying to digest a steak
at 4:00 p.m.

her seven-year-old,
asked what he'd like to become,
replies, *A boss*

a Jew eating ham
hoping his deceased father
isn't watching

German scholar
listens to The Grateful Dead
while rereading *Faust*

bored teenaged genius
showing off his report card …
all A's and F's

mother of six
trying to recall a day
without laundry

golf pro's daughter …
alone, playing happily
in a sand trap

at ninety-three
tasting pumpernickel
for the first time

former beauty queen
pondering the cleft palate
of her baby girl

a bearded elder
teaching his great-grandson
how to shave

televised soccer …
their collie chasing the ball
across a wide screen

a five-year-old boy
screaming in a restaurant,
Dad used the F word

hapless homeowner
elated that his daughter
married a plumber

interfaith home …
their son dying Easter eggs
before the seder

old woman ~ winded
after lifting her frail legs
above a foot stool

multi-pierced teen
criticizing his father
for his taste in suits

tax filing deadline …
outside the post office,
finding two nickels

their three-year-old
convinced that brown *M&Ms*
taste better than red

obese woman …
the flowers on her blouse
about to burst

an accordion
at the base of his backpack …
ninth grade term paper

ancient Greek scholars
swapping their favorite
Yiddish proverbs

in an ER
with food poisoning …
Paris honeymoon

his grandfather
trying to persuade him
that novels are cool

her son arguing
that a bag of marshmallows
is, too, a dinner

2:40 a.m. ~
a poet wishing his muse
would quiet down

OCD woman,
her bipolar husband
discuss adoption

a two-year-old boy
and his puppy snacking
on pink *Play-Doh*

midsummer day …
an elderly man spitting
in a wishing well

a sixteen-year-old
wearing a spiked dog collar
to his English class

health food store owner
checking the pants pockets
of his grandchildren

their fourth meeting ~
his psychiatrist asking
for PC advice

circus performer
fighting a panic attack
on the trapeze

backyard hammock …
a chocolate Lab puppy
fully entangled

three men in a bar
watch ladies' figure skating
for the wrong reasons

medieval scholar
asking his teenaged grandson
to define *homie*

an old poor woman
on line in a doughnut shop
eyes the cupped pennies

Jewish matron
teaching her punk granddaughter
the rules of mah-jongg

post bachelor party …
pondering how to explain
his shaved eyebrows

televangelist
wearing lifts and a toupee,
preaching the truth

her six-year-old
fixing breakfast for himself …
Peeps atop *Twinkies*

his kid sister calls
Child Protective Services
post-pinching

old janitor
mopping a floor as he hums
an aria

centenarian
noting it's been three decades
since he combed his hair

St. Patrick's Day …
her Dad singing *Danny Boy*
in Hungarian

a boy practicing
the Heimlich maneuver
on his pet turtle

elderly waiter
struggling to overcome
diminished recall

talentless actor
considers changing his name
to *Oscar Wynn*

grandfather, grandson
wishing they could exchange
wrinkles and pimples

in a deep sleep
a high-powered lawyer
sucking his thumb

with an eraser
a young boy tries to remove
his mother's tattoo

their third session ...
noticing her therapist
has a pierced tongue

ninety-year-old twins ...
the older one still calling
the younger, *Kid*

field hockey star ...
her thighs and shins shaded
red, black, and blue

theater district ...
trying to restrain himself
from slugging a mime

married thirty years
admitting to her husband
she's never climaxed

a six-year-old girl
asking her depressed father
where it hurts

barber shop …
a demented bald man
requests sideburns

March seventeenth …
his son bathing their poodle
in green food dye

Baylor-DePaul game …
relaxed Jews sitting amongst
Baptists, Catholics

school bus driver
withstanding screeching children
and a hangover

post-circus
his daughter requesting
a pet lion

breakfast meeting …
the chairman of the board
dunking *Fig Newtons*

at the beach
an Amish teen receiving
her first wolf-whistle

frigid battlefield …
steam rising from the wound
of a dying man

in his office
wondering which will come first:
tenure or death

Thanksgiving night …
the granddaughters discussing
how to purge

rural driver
uncertain whether a cow
has the right-of-way

math professor
clueless as to the price
of a first-class stamp

from their bedrooms
his two pre-teen daughters
phoning each other

Macular Degeneration

Rather than try
to discern the world
through haze, blind spots,
distortion, and blur,
she prefers to close her lids
and see trees and flowers,
seashores and canyons,
sunrises and snowfalls,
friends and neighbors,
lightning and rainbows,
her children and grandchildren–
all clear as crystal–
in her mind's eye.

sub-zero night ...
invisible, homeless men
sleeping on the street

married three weeks,
learning to apologize
when he's innocent

in church, four brothers
aged five, six, eight, and ten
wearing the same frown

uninsured man
wearing suspenders
and a belt

an eighteen-year-old
spoiling a perfect nose
with a steel stud

bulimic teen
calculating how much food
she's wasted this month

a young priest
requesting permission
to wear an earring

paraplegic man
cursing at the dropped coins
he can't pick up

history teacher
groaning as he circles
anti-semantic

overturned car ...
three birthday balloons floating
over the back seat

old pharmacist
advising a nervous teen
about condoms

a poor Mexican
driving through Beverly Hills
smiles at the excess

roller coaster ride ~
a ten-year-old boy laughing,
his father praying

in his cab
a New York trucker singing
Oklahoma

French restaurant …
their son requests an éclair
for his entree

commemorating
the tenth anniversary
of his third divorce

balding professor
allowing his eyebrows
to sprout wildly

first day of spring …
wearing her new sandals
despite the snow

5/7/05 …
a haiku poet's baby
begins her first day

pre-prom ~ his daughter
choosing the most garish gown
in Massachusetts

Orthodox Jew
worried his meal tastes too good
to be kosher

therapy client
removing all makeup
before her session

longtime waitress
insisting that new patrons
call her *Mom*

high school senior
choosing amongst colleges
based on their mascots

celiac patient
wistfully remembering
the taste of rye bread

Creativity arises out of the tension between spontaneity and limitations, the latter (like the river banks) forcing the spontaneity into the various forms which are essential to the work of art or poem.

Rollo May

ADHD teen
attempting to wallpaper
her bedroom

hysterical Mom
trying to calm her baby
locked in the car

upscale bookstore …
a student reading *Macbeth*
over a peach scone

on his sister's dare
a seven-year-old boy
eating blue cheese

demented elder
mistaking her great-grandson
for her kid brother

chief executive
asking the maid to purchase
his *Cocoa Puffs*

kindergarten class …
two Brookes, two Jades, three Ambers,
not one Mary

moving day ~ her son
mailing change-of-address cards
to Gramps and Santa

senryu poet
visits a tattoo parlor
for material

weeping teenager
stroking the deep, jagged scratch
on her new car

at a cookout
a vegan sits by the steaks
breathing in deeply

two Jewish mothers
discussing the benefits
of shame and guilt

a five-year-old
asking if petroleum
is just for jelly

early August …
reconsidering college
as he's laying brick

tuxedo-clad man
looking ill upon hearing
'Til death do us part

elderly driver
going around and around
a traffic circle

anxious defendant
observing his lawyer
ogling a juror

young physician
practices writing his name
as a blur

Muslim cab driver
scandalized by the language
of his foul-mouthed fare

outside a classroom
a high school freshman sobbing
before his midterm

drafting her vita
an ex-porn star considers
her references

prepubescent boy
fretting about the size
of his Dad's breasts

recent college grad
orders new stationery
with *B.A.* added

his blind date
claiming she never sweats,
only glistens

grandmother's smile ~
fire-engine red lipstick,
missing front teeth

college football fan
painting the school colors
on his buttocks

their five-year-old
requests that a policeman
lend him his gun

stoic waitress
ignoring peas hurled at her
by twin two-year-olds

asked to describe
her longtime spouse, she replies
Law-abiding

a house divided ...
a combination-lock safe
in each bedroom

during Passover
a Jew ponders which is worse:
eating bread or shrimp

approaching a dwarf
his three-year-old daughter shrieks,
Oompa Loompa!

infant twins' father
inking blue dots on the soles
of one son's feet

after her shift
an old nurse decompressing
with the Marx brothers

little league shortstop
praying that no ground ball
be hit within reach

a French linguist
visiting New York City
jots down the insults

their teenaged son
beginning his senior slump
as a sophomore

3:10 a.m. ~
watching Al Pacino
in *Insomnia*

Easter Sunday …
their daughter musing about
Christ and chocolate

at the altar
a bored bridegroom
stifling a yawn

third-rate writer
blaming his lack of acclaim
on the Zionists

with a stepladder
her nine-year-old practices
basketball dunking

CEO's desk ...
silver-framed photographs
of his three ex-wives

ESL class ...
a student cursing the *ough*
of *though* and *thought*

her Hindu in-laws
shrieking over the meat
in their pea soup

on the beach
their children playing checkers
with shells, bottle caps

funeral service …
a boy and his uncle
thumb-wrestling

great-grandmother
asking if she may touch
his spiked Mohawk

married six decades …
the husband's hair, snow white;
his wife's, jet black

golf foursome …
each retiree's shirt
a shade of yellow

trying to undo
a month's sins by watching
The Ten Commandments

Bronx graduation …
in a sea of mortarboards,
one Yankee cap

book jacket photo
receives a scathing review
from the author's Mom

a burn victim
hoping for just one day
without gasps, stares

Saudi husband
buying his wife a burqa
through the Internet

Wyoming highway ...
in a truck, going ninety
while reading a map

their nine-year-old
asking whether mustard gas
is caused by *Gulden's*

using sugar cubes
Grandpa teaches his offspring
the rules of craps

before his orals
a doctoral candidate
too shaky to shave

in the front row
a student with a tongue
tattooed on his chin

a day off from school ...
agnostic students observe
their Good Friday

old podiatrist
dreaming of a foot model
in high-heeled sandals

a germ-phobic man
fighting a panic attack
after being kissed

Friday the thirteenth ~
one box of Cracker Jack,
two dislodged fillings

an obese mailman
in shorts, dark knee socks, and shoes
ignores the laughter

the night of the prom
his date instructing him
how to change a tire

an English teacher
reducing his waiter's tip
for poor grammar

fastidious Dad
attempting to part and comb
his baby's twelve hairs

depressing birthday …
receiving his first book
with no pictures

V.A. hospital …
three psychiatrists swapping
Bush/Cheney jokes

having crammed all night
a freshman, midterm in hand,
snoring quietly

their son's decision
to become a street mime
evokes screams, swears

on his deathbed
cursing his ex for selling
their *IBM* stock

a Catholic boy
having his first nightmare
about stigmata

prison mess hall ...
thieves, frauds, and embezzlers
sharing their knowledge

an estranged son
learns of his Dad's funeral
two days too late

church collection plate …
three newly minted C-notes
from the hood's loan shark

Sunday evening
in his government office
smoking a joint

a poetess
struggling to pare down
a bloated haiku

a three-year-old's Mom
ponders why he stuffed his ears
with peanut butter

grad school applicant
asked what he likes to read
replies, *On line?*

an eighth grader
surfs the Internet, searching
for foreign curse words

acrophobic man
begins to feel the jitters
hearing the word *Alp*

family road trip …
counting the number of times
her grandmother groans

a nine-year-old girl
adding to her Christmas list
A boyfriend

The two most engaging powers of an author: new things are made familiar, and familiar things are made new.

Samuel Johnson

We write to taste life twice, in the moment and in retrospection.

Anais Nin

beleaguered father
giving his daughters two hours
per outlet store

paging the realtor …
his wife adores the house,
hates the street name

turnpike rest stop …
insisting that her husband
use the bathroom

teenaged Goth
appreciating the style
of a nun's habit

his seven-year-old
asking whether mannequins
have nipples

Miami Beach …
a woman with dementia
adjusts her earmuffs

his psychologist
quoting *Seinfeld* characters
more often than Freud

Jewish ten-year-old
wonders if smelling bacon
is a sin

inner city …
an Evangelical church
beside a laundrette

his ex-wife's lisp
echoing once again
in his ears

trying to recall
the last time her depressed son
laughed out loud

watching his girlfriend
use newly manicured nails
to split a crab leg

sending off his child
with a new credit card
and a prayer

at the Preakness
two hairdressers picking
the prettiest tail

her son, asleep
wrapped in a beige blanket,
resembling a blintz

on vacation
in a Death Valley resort
reading *Jaws*

enraged father
punching the six-year-old boy
who pinched his daughter

Daytona Beach …
an obese husband and wife
belittling thin folks

a Marine's daughter
getting a henna tattoo
of a bald eagle

Passover's third night …
a Queens bagel store owner
flying to Cancun

a six-year-old boy
and his great-grandmother
trade their fallen teeth

champion swimmer
wearing gold flip-flops
to the White House

fast food carry-out …
a squirrel bounds up a tree,
a fry in its mouth

bald-headed elder
teaching his hair-challenged sons
the comb-over

a grieving child
wondering whether hamsters
go to heaven

old Bostonian
demanding that his grandsons
despise the Yankees

on a salesman's desk
a framed photo of a *Porsche*
that isn't his

post-vacation
a haiku poet yearning
for a spark

in a storm cellar
holding her sleeping baby,
a cyclone above

unhelpful sales clerk
offers an irked customer,
Have a nice day

her three-year-old
rejects the asparagus ...
no hollandaise

New York tourist
leaving an empty beer can
in the Grand Canyon

his vintage sedan ...
Win With Willkie affixed
to its rear bumper

baseball manager ...
his line-up card filled with names
ending in *ez*

old-fashioned father
using his spit to flatten
a son's cowlick

her new son-in-law
noting he does not believe
in underwear

on the expressway
spotting a mangled car
with his wife's plates

Yom Kippur morning ...
a Jewish couple eating
behind closed curtains

little leaguer
using his catcher's mitt
as a throw pillow

a hole in his sock ...
a professor applies
ink to his ankle

young soccer goalie
shuffling back home alone ~
wet, bruised, crying

a Brooklyn boy
eating his morning oatmeal
with last night's chopsticks

her prom night …
stepping out of the limo
into a hailstorm

explains to his son
why the family moved west:
Someone got shot

first-time shoplifter …
her fear of getting caught
dwarfing any thrill

finding their niche ...
neighborhood boys attending
Christian skateboard camp

movie night ...
three policemen enjoying
Scarface

movie night ...
four criminals relishing
Serpico

teenager's father
suffering motion sickness
from her mood swings

Father's Day eve ...
pondering what to get
her blind, senile Dad

after a hard day
listening to his daughter
mangle the oboe

M.B.A. student
flossing furiously
before his orals

trying to save gas
he turns down the radio
in his minivan

beloved elder
tells her grandkids what she hates
about their parents

a police captain
fantasizes committing
the perfect heist

middle-aged woman
noticing how much her spouse
looks like their bulldog

reunion …
unable to get beyond
his uncle's earring

abusive parents
naming their new son after
Grandpa Gaylord

in a batting slump
a third baseman considers
children's charities

renowned novelist
re-reading his first book,
finding a typo

math professor's son
holding up four fingers
as he says, *I'm three*

treasuring the eyes
of his favorite cousin ~
one green, one blue

two rottweiler heads
sticking out of the sunroof
of a speeding car

deceased Mets fan ...
his old cap in the playpen
of his great-grandson

small town bus driver
hoping to become someday
a rich man's chauffeur

A person who publishes a book willfully appears before the populace with his pants down.

Edna St. Vincent Millay

I was working on the proof of one of my poems all the morning, and took out a comma. In the afternoon, I put it back again.

Oscar Wilde

Nobel laureate
lecturing to undergrads
in t-shirts, dozing

fifth grade class photo …
the teacher's pet, unaware
of her rabbit ears

English professor
finds one haiku in a sea
of young adult angst

Jewish punk rocker,
half his head shaved, tries to keep
his yarmulke on

GRE morning …
a senior dropping his keys
down a sewer grate

a ten-year-old boy
lighting his first cigarette
at the wrong end

his mother
finding genius in each act
of her grandchild

her teenaged son
cutting an old credit card
into guitar picks

psychotic patients
discussing the oddities
of their doctors

Auschwitz survivor
sharing his wartime stories
with Vietnam vets

Christmas eve ...
a beggar is handed
a fruitcake

his new girlfriend
telling him not to touch her:
It gets me aroused

bulimic student
writing a term paper
on Sudan's famine

parent/teacher night ...
a problem student's mother
cursing a blue streak

senryu writer
struggling at 3:00 a.m. ~
ellipsis or dash

dermatologist
studying the tattooed arms
of his son's girlfriend

Special Olympics ...
a palsied boy rejoicing,
his father sobbing

three preschoolers ...
their pants down by their shoes
at the urinals

his son's pet mouse
cautiously approaching
an old stuffed lion

poor, depressed woman
choosing between hamburger
and Zoloft

mayoral debate …
counting the number of times
frankly is uttered

a rich man's mother
trying to figure from where
his stinginess comes

photographer
urging a toddler to smile
more naturally

vet's office …
as their spaniel is neutered,
three brothers moan

lesbian's father
asserting she can be cured
by the right man

middle school bee ...
asked to spell the word *sirloin*,
a butcher's child smiles

at the racetrack
an old man falling in love
with a three-year-old

four beagles
in a suburban kennel,
all named Snoopy

a renowned scholar
insulting his students
in Icelandic

couples therapist
treating an anxious man
and his manic dog

their twelve-year-old
offering her third *My bad*
before breakfast

a Hebrew School class
appeals to the Mets' owner
for kosher franks

first-year grad student
practices calling himself
Professor

wishing he had
a different birth month, day …
9/11 boy

his wife's father
viewing New York and Israel
as synonymous

an upscale teen
searching for a handbag
to match her puppy

midnight, in prison ...
a man with a life sentence
besieged by what-ifs

Boston socialist
bemoans his child's expenses
at private school

a ten-year-old girl
not deigning to pick up
a dime on the curb

elderly priest
concerned about misspelling
Deuteronomy

high school recital ...
dancers striving for sexy,
achieve peculiar

new father holding
mentally retarded twins,
anticipating

hot summer evening ...
three sisters, mid-period,
sharing one bathroom

post-rhinoplasty ...
her black eyes evoke concern
about spouse abuse

south Miami ...
a rage-filled driver
draws a machete

at the M.V.A.
a man in a tuxedo
awaits his photo

Berkeley faculty …
more men than women
in ponytails

dining with his son,
searching for some semblance
of himself

a therapist frets
over a depressed client
missing for two days

pugnacious chemist
showing off his new dog ~
half-boxer, half-Lab

thirtieth birthday …
wishing his wife won't become
her mother

at the market
two of his students notice
prunes in his cart

trying to find
a prom dress that doesn't clash
with her tattoo

the band playing
It's Hard Out Here for a Pimp …
wedding cocktail hour

outside their school
scores of students picketing
for sugared sodas

uptown bar …
his blind date drinking bock beer
from a bottle

a lawyer writing
to his pro bono clients
he's lost his lease

four-year-old twins
playing a game of ring-toss
with Mom's hoop earrings

young psychiatrist
catching his new patient
in another lie

a Jewish comic
wearing a porkpie hat
to synagogue

owner of four cats
considers claiming *PetSmart*
as a dependant

graduation day …
a blind, spastic teen getting
thunderous applause

a burly trucker
in a greasy spoon, asks for
ham on rye, no crusts

the Hoyle family
resisting the urge to name
their baby, Olive

pre-wedding, the groom
scraping from his car's bumper
an obscene sticker

psychoanalyst
buying a box of cigars
on Freud's birthday

Little Italy ...
Rocco's Confectionery
intrigues the tourists

family dinner ...
vegan parents and children
and three depressed pets

their Mom's funeral ...
each estranged child wearing
a shade of red

a nine-year-old cook
using slices of white bread
as potholders

classics professor
refusing to read or watch
the local news

Utah leftist
seeing a psychiatrist
for loneliness

outdoor commencement …
a provost wipes from his gown
avian droppings

an eight-year-old boy
feeling gypped that his birthday
falls on Mother's Day

burned-out therapist
mulling a career shift
to dog training

senior prom eve …
praying that rain does not
undo her updo

next-door neighbors …
the *Welcome* on their doormat
faces the wrong way

a middle-aged man
noting he's a few cans short
of six-pack abs

a surgeon's son
celebrates acquiring
his hack license

middle school teacher
judging students' haiku
by syllable count

at age seventy
choosing to change legally
her hated first name

telling his girlfriend
it was he who invented
cherry dental floss

a stevedore
running into his foreman
at a day spa

schizophrenic boy
using only black crayons
to draw a sunrise

a country club
proudly accepting its first
Jewish caddie

Index of Poems' Original Sources

Some of the poems presented in this volume have been published or are "in press" elsewhere. Listed below are the titles of these poems and the journals in which they have appeared or soon will appear.

In **Food, Culture, and Society: An International Journal of Multidisciplinary Research:** *health food store owner; her son arguing*

In **Hummingbird: Magazine of the Short Poem:** *an English teacher; parent/teacher night*

In **The Pegasus Review:** *grandfather, grandson; mother of six; with an eraser*

Author's Note

Born and raised in New York City, Dr. Robert H. Deluty now lives in Ellicott City, Maryland with his wife, Barbara, and their children, Laura and David. He has been a psychology professor at the University of Maryland, Baltimore County since 1980. He was named UMBC's Presidential Teaching Professor in 2002 and is currently the Director of the Clinical Psychology Doctoral Program. He teaches undergraduate and graduate courses in abnormal psychology, psychological assessment, and therapeutic interventions. *Infinity in the Palm of One's Hand* is his ninth book.